Question a Day
JOURNAL

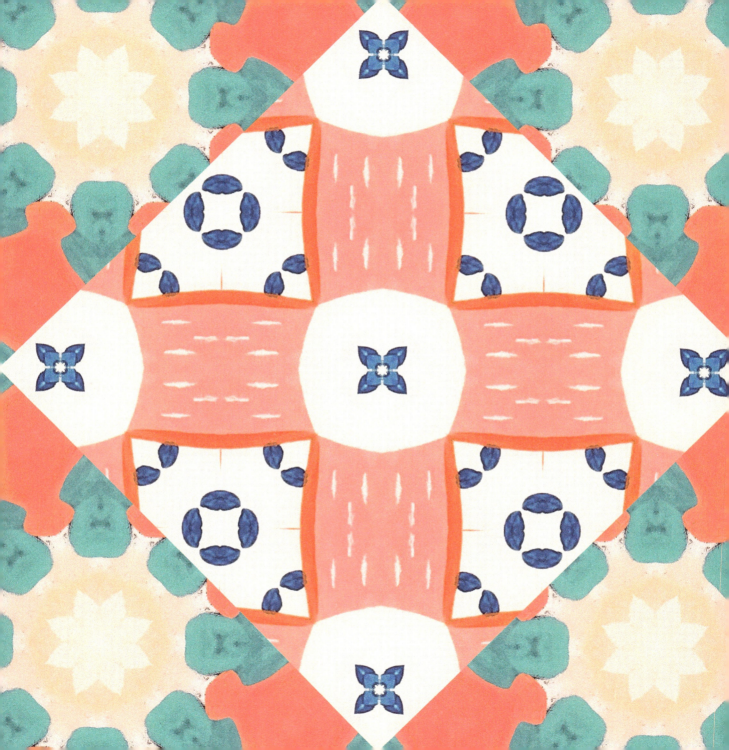

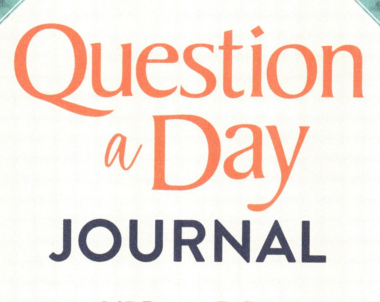

Question a Day

JOURNAL

365 Days to Reflect and Express Yourself

JACLYN MUSSELMAN

ROCKRIDGE PRESS

For general information on our other products and services, please contact our Customer Care Department within the United States at (866) 744-2665, or outside the United States at (510) 253-0500.

Hardcover ISBN: 979-8-88608-015-5
Paperback ISBN: 978-1-68539-808-8

Manufactured in the United States of America

Interior and Cover Designer: John Calmeyer
Art Producer: Janice Ackerman
Editor: Chloe Moffett
Production Manager: Riley Hoffman

Illustrations © Julia Dreams/Creative Market.

10 9 8 7 6 5 4 3 2 1 0

This journal belongs to

_____

Introduction

Journaling has long been a meaningful part of my life. When I was a teenager, my mother and I started a journal practice that included writing notes back and forth to each other. This was a comfortable and fun way for us to communicate throughout my high school years. The experience made a lasting impression on me, and I have integrated journaling into my daily life ever since.

As a longtime fan of journaling, but also as a counselor, I know the importance of pausing for self-reflection. Journaling provides that opportunity, but starting a journal can be overwhelming. You might wonder what to write about, how much to write, and how often you should make a new entry. You might have written in a journal in the past only to abandon it after a few weeks or months. I wrote this book, with a year's worth of stimulating prompts, to help you get started.

In the hectic pace of today's world, we often forget to stop and take time to be in our own minds. But these intentional pauses can be flexible and are so beneficial. As a busy mom and wife, I have few moments alone each day. I use some of that time to journal because I have found that by documenting the little details in my life, I am able to be grateful and to stay in a positive mindset.

I encourage you to incorporate journaling whenever you have time in your day. Even just a few minutes of journaling can have a big impact on your present mood and attitude about the future! I believe that spending a moment to write in your journal will give you a more positive outlook on the day. Then, when you can look back on your thoughts and experiences over days, weeks, and months, you will get a better idea of what you want your future life to look like.

How to Use This Book

This 365-day journal is designed to make journaling easy for you. You will answer one prompt or question each day for the entire year. The prompts are categorized into five different themes that will ensure you stay engaged with journaling and inspired to contemplate every aspect of your life:

 Looking Back: Reflect on your past—from the small details in life to big-picture changes.

 Self-Discovery: Reflect on your unique, individual journey to become more aware of your authentic self.

 Gratitude and Positive Thinking: Express appreciation for what you have or experiences that have shaped who you are.

 Just for Fun: Recall and write about the funny events of everyday life and reveal a less serious side of yourself.

 Looking Forward: Explore your dreams, hopes, and goals for the future.

You can start the journal at any time. Simply flip to the current date and start writing! If it's possible, I suggest deciding on a specific time each day to write in your journal. This can be helpful for establishing journaling as a regular practice, and you will be more likely to remember to journal if you have a set routine. Don't worry if you miss a day—you can go back and fill it in when you have time. If a particular journal prompt does not speak to you that day, go on to a different prompt or just write down what is on your mind.

This is your journal, so do what works best for you. After a year, you will have a written collection of personal thoughts and dreams. You can save this journal and look back at your reflections for years to come. Maybe someday you will want to pass the journal on to your family to help them learn more about you.

1 What are your goals for the coming year? What are the specific steps you need to take to reach each goal?

_____

_____

_____

_____

_____

_____

_____

2 Write about a situation in the past year when you experienced self-doubt. How did you overcome this feeling?

_____

_____

_____

_____

_____

_____

_____

3 Document a typical day in your life. Write about what you do in the morning, afternoon, evening, and night. What does your routine look like?

_____

_____

_____

_____

_____

_____

_____

4 List ten positive things that you are grateful for in your life.

_____

_____

_____

_____

_____

_____

_____

_____

5 What is one personal quality or behavior that you would like to improve upon? What can you do to make this happen?

_____

_____

_____

_____

_____

_____

_____

6 Do you feel like the best years of your life are still to come? Why or why not?

_____

_____

_____

_____

_____

_____

_____

7 If you could relive one day in your life, what day would that be? Would you do anything differently on that day?

_____

_____

_____

_____

_____

_____

8 What do you do to recharge after a stressful day?

_____

_____

_____

_____

_____

_____

_____

9 How do you like to celebrate your birthday?

_____

_____

_____

_____

_____

_____

_____

10 What do you love about your own body?

_____

_____

_____

_____

_____

_____

_____

11 What has been the most difficult time period in your life? How did you cope with that challenging season?

_____

_____

_____

_____

_____

_____

12 What is something new you would like to learn? What could you do to gain more knowledge?

_____

_____

_____

_____

_____

_____

_____

13 If you were given one week of the year to do anything you wanted and your budget was not a concern, what would you do?

_____

_____

_____

_____

_____

_____

_____

14 What do you love about this time of year? What do you like to do during these months?

_____

_____

_____

_____

_____

_____

_____

15 Write about a time in your life in which you wanted to give up but kept trying. Did you reach the desired outcome?

_____

_____

_____

_____

_____

_____

_____

16 What makes you feel cozy and safe?

_____

_____

_____

_____

_____

_____

_____

17 Describe one of the best days from the past year.

_____

_____

_____

_____

_____

_____

_____

18 Describe something that has been bothering you lately. Do you think you will care about it in a month? A year? Five years from now?

_____

_____

_____

_____

_____

_____

_____

19 What is your favorite book of all time? Who is the author and what is the book about?

_____

_____

_____

_____

_____

_____

_____

20 If you were given the chance to know how your life will turn out, would you want to know every single detail? Why or why not?

_____

_____

_____

_____

_____

_____

_____

21 What was the last compliment you received? Who gave you the compliment? How did it make you feel?

_____

_____

_____

_____

_____

_____

_____

22 Describe a time when you shared some exciting news with someone. How did they react to the news? How did you feel about sharing it?

_____

_____

_____

_____

_____

_____

_____

23 How would people close to you describe you as a person?

_____

_____

_____

_____

_____

_____

_____

24 Who makes up your support system? What does each person do to support you?

_____

_____

_____

_____

_____

_____

_____

25 What is one of your hidden talents? Do people know about this talent? Why or why not?

_____

_____

_____

_____

_____

_____

_____

26 What is one of the best experiences you have had in your life? Describe the details of the experience and how it made you feel.

_____

_____

_____

_____

_____

_____

_____

27 What do you struggle to love most about yourself? How can you improve your self-love?

_____

_____

_____

_____

_____

_____

_____

28 What are ten simple pleasures you are grateful for?

_____

_____

_____

_____

_____

_____

_____

29 Write down five things that are on your bucket list. Indicate when you hope to accomplish or experience each of these.

_____

_____

_____

_____

_____

_____

_____

30 Are you where you imagined you would be at this point in your life? Are there aspects of your life that are better or worse than you expected?

_____

_____

_____

_____

_____

_____

_____

31 Who is an important person from your past that you have not talked to in a long time? Could you reach out to them soon?

_____

_____

_____

_____

_____

_____

_____

1 What is your favorite holiday? What makes it so special?

_____

_____

_____

_____

_____

_____

2 What makes you happy to be alive? How can you bring more of that into your life every day?

_____

_____

_____

_____

_____

_____

3 How would you describe the place where you grew up? How did your hometown shape who you are today?

_____

_____

_____

_____

_____

_____

_____

4 Where would you like to be financially in five years? What steps are you taking now to achieve those goals?

_____

_____

_____

_____

_____

_____

_____

5 Do you consider yourself an introvert or an extrovert? What personal characteristics or traits make you one or the other?

_____

_____

_____

_____

_____

_____

_____

6 Write about a person with whom you always have fun. What are some of your favorite ways to spend time with this person?

_____

_____

_____

_____

_____

_____

_____

7 What are some of your family's annual traditions that you are looking forward to celebrating this year?

_____

_____

_____

_____

_____

_____

_____

8 Describe your dream house. Where would it be located? What would it look like on the inside and outside?

_____

_____

_____

_____

_____

_____

_____

9 What is one risk you wish you had taken in the past? Could you still take that risk now?

_____

_____

_____

_____

_____

_____

10 If you were to change your career, what would you do? What could you do now to make your current career more satisfying?

_____

_____

_____

_____

_____

_____

_____

11 When was the last time you complimented someone? How do you think that made them feel? How did it make you feel?

_____

_____

_____

_____

_____

_____

_____

12 What is one of your most treasured possessions? Why is it so special?

_____

_____

_____

_____

_____

_____

_____

13 Do you have positive memories from your childhood? Share a few here.

_____

_____

_____

_____

_____

_____

_____

14 Write about your favorite person and name all their good qualities.

_____

_____

_____

_____

_____

_____

_____

15 Would you rather be lucky or wise? Why?

_____

_____

_____

_____

_____

_____

16 What are five positive things in your life right now?

_____

_____

_____

_____

_____

_____

17 What is a personal achievement in your life that you had to work hard for? How did you achieve it?

_____

_____

_____

_____

_____

_____

_____

18 Is there a relationship in your life that you need to improve? What can you do to work on that relationship?

_____

_____

_____

_____

_____

_____

_____

19 Write about the place you call home.

_____

_____

_____

_____

_____

_____

_____

20 How do you let others know you love them? Do you think they know you love them?

_____

_____

_____

_____

_____

_____

_____

21 Do you worry a lot? How do you manage worry and anxiety?

_____

_____

_____

_____

_____

_____

_____

22 How did you grow as a person last year?

_____

_____

_____

_____

_____

_____

_____

23 What would be the title of your autobiography? Why?

_____

_____

_____

_____

_____

_____

24 What can you do this week to help someone who could use your support?

_____

_____

_____

_____

_____

_____

25 Did you set any New Year's goals? If so, how are they going right now? How will you continue to reach your goals this year?

_____

_____

_____

_____

_____

_____

_____

26 What is one situation in your life that seemed bad at the time but ended up working out for you?

_____

_____

_____

_____

_____

_____

_____

27 When was the last time you felt really relaxed? Describe how you felt.

_____

_____

_____

_____

_____

_____

_____

28 What was the last dream you can remember?

_____

_____

_____

_____

_____

_____

_____

_____

29 What will you do with this extra day this year?

_____

_____

_____

_____

_____

_____

_____

1 Describe the worst breakup you have had with a friend or a partner. How did you heal from it?

_____

_____

_____

_____

_____

_____

2 What is a challenging skill or hobby you have wanted to master? Is there something preventing you from trying to learn this skill or hobby?

_____

_____

_____

_____

_____

_____

3 What are some personal health goals you are working toward right now? What steps are you taking to meet your goals?

_____

_____

_____

_____

_____

_____

_____

4 Which actor would you want to play you in a movie and why? What genre of movie would it be?

_____

_____

_____

_____

_____

_____

_____

5 Have you accomplished any of your childhood dreams? Why or why not? Do those dreams still align with your current dreams and goals?

_____

_____

_____

_____

_____

_____

6 Where did you notice beauty this week?

_____

_____

_____

_____

_____

_____

_____

7 When you are in a bad mood, what makes you feel better?

_____

_____

_____

_____

_____

_____

_____

8 What do you hope to accomplish by the end of the year?

_____

_____

_____

_____

_____

_____

_____

9 Think about someone who has been a positive role model in your life. What would you tell them about how they have helped you?

_____

_____

_____

_____

_____

_____

_____

10 If you were given the opportunity to spend a day with a deceased relative or ancestor, who would you choose and why?

_____

_____

_____

_____

_____

_____

_____

11 What is your earliest childhood memory?

_____

_____

_____

_____

_____

_____

12 What motto or quote do you live by or find inspiring? What does it mean to you?

_____

_____

_____

_____

_____

_____

_____

13 What is your favorite creative outlet? How can it improve your mood?

_____

_____

_____

_____

_____

_____

_____

14 What is your favorite pet, past or present? If you've never had a pet, would you like to? Why or why not?

_____

_____

_____

_____

_____

_____

_____

15 What is the most exhilarating experience you've had this year?

_____

_____

_____

_____

_____

_____

_____

16 In what ways do you consider yourself lucky?

_____

_____

_____

_____

_____

_____

_____

17 Name two or three good things that happened to you this week.

_____

_____

_____

_____

_____

_____

_____

18 Name five of your core values. How do you live your life by these?

_____

_____

_____

_____

_____

_____

_____

19 What is the best meal you have had recently? What did you like about it? Will you have it again soon?

_____

_____

_____

_____

_____

_____

20 How do you feel about aging? Are there aspects of aging that are difficult for you to accept?

_____

_____

_____

_____

_____

_____

21 What does the word "mindfulness" mean to you? How do you practice mindfulness in your life?

_____

_____

_____

_____

_____

_____

_____

22 If you got to spend an entire day all by yourself doing anything you wanted, what would you do?

_____

_____

_____

_____

_____

_____

_____

23 What is one thing you can do now that can help make the world a better place for future generations?

_____

_____

_____

_____

_____

_____

_____

24 What is one piece of advice you did not take but wish you had?

_____

_____

_____

_____

_____

_____

_____

25 What are your biggest strengths? What are some specific examples of when or how these strengths have helped you in life?

_____

_____

_____

_____

_____

_____

_____

26 What are your biggest weaknesses? What are some examples of how these weaknesses have been problematic in your life?

_____

_____

_____

_____

_____

_____

_____

27 When will you next have an opportunity to meet new people? Will you try to connect with someone in that situation? Why or why not?

_____

_____

_____

_____

_____

_____

_____

28 What aspects of your life are better now than they were a year ago?

_____

_____

_____

_____

_____

_____

_____

29 What role does social media play in your life? How do you feel about it and why?

_____

_____

_____

_____

_____

_____

_____

30 Do you feel any pressure in your life from your family, job, or yourself? How are you dealing with that pressure?

_____

_____

_____

_____

_____

_____

_____

31 When was the last time you cried? What was the catalyst?

_____

_____

_____

_____

_____

_____

_____

1 If money were no object, what is the most indulgent thing you would buy?

_____

_____

_____

_____

_____

_____

2 What are some things you are looking forward to doing this month?

_____

_____

_____

_____

_____

_____

3 Is there someone in your life that you need to forgive right now? Are you willing to forgive them?

_____

_____

_____

_____

_____

_____

_____

4 If you could go back and give advice to your teenage self, what would you say? Do you think you would take this advice?

_____

_____

_____

_____

_____

_____

_____

5 What is your favorite way to start the day?

_____

_____

_____

_____

_____

_____

_____

6 If you could rewrite an event in world history, which one would you choose? How would you change the outcome?

_____

_____

_____

_____

_____

_____

_____

7 If you did not have to worry about people's opinions or your own finances, what could you do with your life?

_____

_____

_____

_____

_____

_____

_____

8 Which of your qualities has helped you deal with life's ups and downs? Name a time when a specific trait got you through a situation.

_____

_____

_____

_____

_____

_____

_____

9 Has something bad happened to you recently? Did anything good come of it? What did you learn from it?

_____

_____

_____

_____

_____

_____

10 What are five things you love about where you live?

_____

_____

_____

_____

_____

_____

11 What food makes you think of home? Do you have a specific memory about this food?

_____

_____

_____

_____

_____

_____

_____

12 What do you imagine your life will be like in five years?

_____

_____

_____

_____

_____

_____

_____

13 When was the last time you did a random act of kindness? How did you feel about doing it, and how did the person react?

_____

_____

_____

_____

_____

_____

_____

14 What are your feelings toward your parents?

_____

_____

_____

_____

_____

_____

_____

15 What are some of your biggest fears? Have these fears changed over the years?

_____

_____

_____

_____

_____

_____

_____

16 Are you willing to confront your fears? Why or why not?

_____

_____

_____

_____

_____

_____

_____

17 Would you rather spend a week in a mountain cabin or at a tropical beach resort? Why would you like one better than the other?

_____

_____

_____

_____

_____

_____

_____

18 What is one vacation you hope to go on in the next five years? What will you do on this trip? Who will you take with you?

_____

_____

_____

_____

_____

_____

_____

19 Are you good at time management? Why or why not?

_____

_____

_____

_____

_____

_____

_____

20 How have you changed in the past decade?

_____

_____

_____

_____

_____

_____

_____

21 When do you feel most at peace? How often do you have these feelings of peace? How can you have more moments like this?

_____

_____

_____

_____

_____

_____

_____

22 What book are you currently reading or which TV show are you watching? What interests you most about it?

_____

_____

_____

_____

_____

_____

_____

23 What do you like the most about the spring season? What are your favorite things to do in the spring?

_____

_____

_____

_____

_____

_____

24 Write about the worst job you have ever had. What made this job so awful? What did you learn from the experience?

_____

_____

_____

_____

_____

_____

25 Describe your favorite job. What were the best aspects of this job?

_____

_____

_____

_____

_____

_____

_____

26 Write about something you accomplished this week. How did it make you feel?

_____

_____

_____

_____

_____

_____

_____

27
Do you think you have self-confidence? When do you feel most confident?

_____

_____

_____

_____

_____

_____

_____

28
What is the most important thing to focus on today?

_____

_____

_____

_____

_____

_____

_____

29 Name five things that make you extraordinary.

_____

_____

_____

_____

_____

_____

30 What are some good or bad habits you have that affect your well-being?

_____

_____

_____

_____

_____

_____

_____

1 How do you know you are appreciated?

_____

_____

_____

_____

_____

_____

2 Write about someone you love who is no longer a part of your life. What do you miss the most about them?

_____

_____

_____

_____

_____

_____

_____

3 Write about one of your quirks or unique habits.

_____

_____

_____

_____

_____

_____

_____

4 If you were given ten million dollars as a gift, what would you do with all the money?

_____

_____

_____

_____

_____

_____

_____

5 What is your favorite way to spend a Friday night? How often do you get to spend your Fridays this way?

_____

_____

_____

_____

_____

_____

_____

6 What is an opinion you have held in the past that you have changed your mind on recently? Why have you changed your stance?

_____

_____

_____

_____

_____

_____

_____

7 What is your purpose right now? How has it changed this year?

_____

_____

_____

_____

_____

_____

_____

8 What does the word "brave" mean to you? Share some examples of when you have been brave in the past.

_____

_____

_____

_____

_____

_____

_____

9 What is one of your biggest pet peeves? How do you manage the situation when you have to deal with this pet peeve?

_____

_____

_____

_____

_____

_____

10 What can you do today that will bring you joy?

_____

_____

_____

_____

_____

_____

11 Describe a frightening experience in your life and how you got through it.

_____

_____

_____

_____

_____

_____

12 When was a time you had to deal with failure? How did you handle the situation?

_____

_____

_____

_____

_____

_____

_____

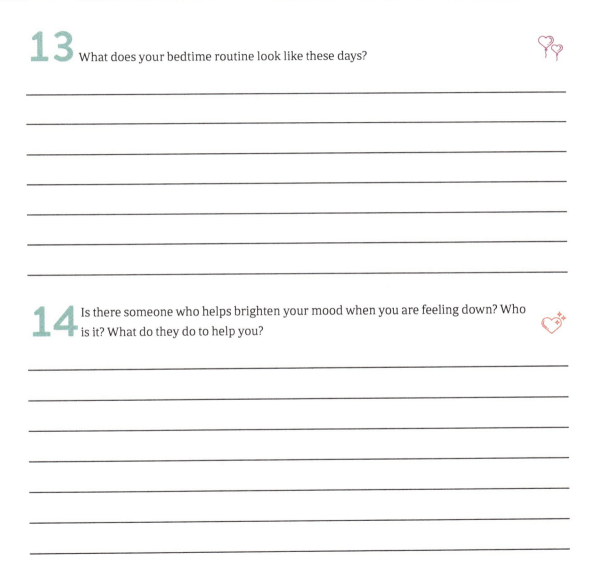

13 What does your bedtime routine look like these days?

_____

_____

_____

_____

_____

_____

_____

14 Is there someone who helps brighten your mood when you are feeling down? Who is it? What do they do to help you?

_____

_____

_____

_____

_____

_____

_____

15 What aspect of your future do you worry about most? Why?

_____

_____

_____

_____

_____

_____

16 What is one of the best vacations you have taken in your life? What are some of your favorite moments from that trip?

_____

_____

_____

_____

_____

_____

17 Name one or two songs that bring you a lot of memories. What are the specific memories?

_____

_____

_____

_____

_____

_____

18 When you are feeling sad, what are some things you do to make yourself feel better?

_____

_____

_____

_____

_____

_____

_____

19 When have you given up on something and it was the right decision? How did you know it was the right choice?

_____

_____

_____

_____

_____

_____

_____

20 At this time of year, what do you love most about where you live? Do you have any favorite plants that are blooming?

_____

_____

_____

_____

_____

_____

_____

21 Write about the last time you were in nature. Describe the scene. What positive feelings did you have about being there?

_____

_____

_____

_____

_____

_____

_____

22 Did you have a good relationship with your parents when you were a teenager? Why or why not?

_____

_____

_____

_____

_____

_____

_____

23 When is the next time you get to relax? What do you plan to do?

_____

_____

_____

_____

_____

_____

_____

24 Is there someone in your life you need to ask for forgiveness? What can you do now to ask for their forgiveness?

_____

_____

_____

_____

_____

_____

_____

25 What are five things you love about your family or friends?

_____

_____

_____

_____

_____

_____

26 What is the biggest risk you have ever taken in your life? How did it work out for you?

_____

_____

_____

_____

_____

_____

27

Describe your personality as a child. Do you have a similar personality now?

_____

_____

_____

_____

_____

_____

28

What is something you hope to not be worrying about next year?

_____

_____

_____

_____

_____

_____

_____

29 Do you think you are an inspiration to anyone? What qualities do you possess that are inspiring?

_____

_____

_____

_____

_____

_____

30 Write about one or two life events that helped shape you into who you are today. Were these life events you expected to have?

_____

_____

_____

_____

_____

_____

31 What is something you love doing but have not had the time to do recently? What is keeping you from that activity?

_____

_____

_____

_____

_____

_____

_____

1 Describe your best personality trait. How has this trait helped you through life?

_____

_____

_____

_____

_____

_____

_____

2 What is coming up this week that you are dreading? What can you do to make this activity or task more pleasant?

_____

_____

_____

_____

_____

_____

_____

3 Write about a cause or charity that is important to you. Why does it mean so much to you?

_____

_____

_____

_____

_____

_____

_____

4 When was the last time you were asked to keep a secret? Are you still keeping this secret?

_____

_____

_____

_____

_____

_____

_____

5 Describe your favorite meal.

_____

_____

_____

_____

_____

_____

_____

6 What does your dream life look like? Do you feel like you are living it?

_____

_____

_____

_____

_____

_____

_____

_____

7 What is one goal you have for yourself for the next five years? What are some specific actions you are taking to reach this goal?

_____

_____

_____

_____

_____

_____

_____

8 What are five things in your home that bring you joy and why?

_____

_____

_____

_____

_____

_____

_____

9 When was the last time you laughed really hard?

_____

_____

_____

_____

_____

_____

_____

10 Write about a big fight you had with someone important in your life. Were you and the other person able to forgive each other? Why or why not?

_____

_____

_____

_____

_____

_____

_____

11 How can you overcome your self-doubt?

_____

_____

_____

_____

_____

_____

12 Do you have any bad habits you need to break? What actions can you take this month to try to break these habits?

_____

_____

_____

_____

_____

_____

13 Who has unconditionally supported you in your life? Name a time this person helped you through a particular challenge.

_____

_____

_____

_____

_____

_____

14 Who inspires you most? In what ways does this person inspire you?

_____

_____

_____

_____

_____

_____

15 Name your childhood best friends. What are some of your memories of these friendships?

_____

_____

_____

_____

_____

_____

_____

16 Would you rather spend a day back in time 100 years ago or spend a day in the future 100 years from now? What do you think that day would look like?

_____

_____

_____

_____

_____

_____

_____

17 What is the best advice you have ever received? Who gave you the advice? Did you take it?

_____

_____

_____

_____

_____

_____

_____

18 What kind of legacy do you want to leave behind? How do you want people to remember you?

_____

_____

_____

_____

_____

_____

_____

19 What is the best gift you have ever given another person?

_____

_____

_____

_____

_____

_____

20 What was something you were not excited about doing recently that ended up not being as bad as you imagined?

_____

_____

_____

_____

_____

_____

21 If you could live anywhere in the world right now, where would it be? What makes you want to live in this place?

_____

_____

_____

_____

_____

_____

_____

22 Do you ever feel misunderstood? Why do you think people misunderstand you? What can you do to help people know you better?

_____

_____

_____

_____

_____

_____

_____

23 When people come to you for help, what do they usually want help with?

_____

_____

_____

_____

_____

_____

24 Do you feel like you've "made it" in life? Why or why not?

_____

_____

_____

_____

_____

_____

25 Describe the most thrill-seeking experience you have ever had. What were you feeling at the time? Would you ever do it again?

_____

_____

_____

_____

_____

_____

_____

26 What is your favorite season of the year? What are some of your favorite things to do during that season?

_____

_____

_____

_____

_____

_____

_____

27 Do you consider yourself a happy person? What can you do to bring even more joy into your life?

_____

_____

_____

_____

_____

_____

28 What are three ways you can get out of your comfort zone this year?

_____

_____

_____

_____

_____

_____

29
Name ten things that happened this month that you are grateful for.

_____

_____

_____

_____

_____

_____

30
What are some of your favorite summer memories?

_____

_____

_____

_____

_____

_____

1 Which of the mundane tasks in life are you grateful you can do?

_____

_____

_____

_____

_____

_____

2 When was the last time you laughed so hard it hurt?

_____

_____

_____

_____

_____

_____

_____

3 In what area of your life do you feel the most organized?

_____
_____
_____
_____
_____
_____

4 What in your life would you like to never change?

_____
_____
_____
_____
_____
_____

5 What is one physical thing you own that you could not live without? What would your life look like if you did not have this item?

_____

_____

_____

_____

_____

_____

_____

6 Write about a time when you had a major setback in your life. How did you overcome this challenge?

_____

_____

_____

_____

_____

_____

_____

7 If you could only enjoy one song, one movie, and one book for life, which of each would you choose and why?

_____

_____

_____

_____

_____

_____

_____

8 What relationships are you looking for in life? (This could be relationships with friends, romantic partners, coworkers, or family.)

_____

_____

_____

_____

_____

_____

_____

9 What is the best gift you have ever received?

_____

_____

_____

_____

_____

_____

10 How do you stand out from the crowd?

_____

_____

_____

_____

_____

_____

11 Where is one of the most beautiful places you have been? What are some of the beautiful things about this place?

_____

_____

_____

_____

_____

_____

_____

12 What is your word or motto for the year? If you haven't chosen one, try doing so now. What does it mean to you?

_____

_____

_____

_____

_____

_____

_____

13 When was the last time you tried something new? How did the experience make you feel?

_____

_____

_____

_____

_____

_____

14 Describe the best day you have had recently.

_____

_____

_____

_____

_____

_____

15 How do you feel about your current age? What do you like and not like about being at this point in your life?

_____

_____

_____

_____

_____

_____

_____

16 Who was your first love? What was the experience like, and how did the relationship end?

_____

_____

_____

_____

_____

_____

_____

17 What is the next holiday you are looking forward to? How will you celebrate?

_____

_____

_____

_____

_____

_____

18 What is your least favorite day of the week? Why?

_____

_____

_____

_____

_____

_____

19 What distractions get in the way of you being your most productive?

_____

_____

_____

_____

_____

_____

20 What is the best news you have ever received? How did you process the news?

_____

_____

_____

_____

_____

_____

_____

21 What aspects of your personality do you appreciate the most? Which ones are harder to accept?

_____

_____

_____

_____

_____

_____

_____

22 What takes up significant time and energy in your life now that will not be in your life in five years? How do you feel about that?

_____

_____

_____

_____

_____

_____

_____

23 What are five things in your life that you are happy about right now?

_____

_____

_____

_____

_____

_____

_____

24 What is one of your favorite memories with your family this year? Describe how it made you feel.

_____

_____

_____

_____

_____

_____

_____

25 What is your favorite month of the year? What are some of your favorite things to do during that month?

_____

_____

_____

_____

_____

_____

_____

26 When was the last time you saw your hard work pay off?

_____

_____

_____

_____

_____

_____

_____

27 Who is someone you confide in the most? What situations has this person helped you through in the past year?

_____

_____

_____

_____

_____

_____

28 If you were granted three wishes, what would they be?

_____

_____

_____

_____

_____

_____

29 What are five things you love about your neighborhood?

_____

_____

_____

_____

_____

_____

30 How do you manage stress? What are some good things you do to relieve stress, and what are some unproductive ways you deal with stress?

_____

_____

_____

_____

_____

_____

31 What were some of your favorite hobbies as a child? Do you still enjoy those activities?

_____

_____

_____

_____

_____

_____

_____

AUGUST

1 What great advice have you received that you have passed on to someone else? With whom did you share it, and how was it received?

_____

_____

_____

_____

_____

_____

2 What are five things you can do this week to take care of your health?

_____

_____

_____

_____

_____

_____

_____

3 Write down one memory or moment that you will cherish for the rest of your life.

_____

_____

_____

_____

_____

_____

_____

4 Think about something you do not like about yourself. Are there any positive takeaways from this trait or ways it has served you?

_____

_____

_____

_____

_____

_____

_____

5 Do you have an embarrassing memory that still makes you cringe?

_____

_____

_____

_____

_____

_____

6 Describe your happy place. Write about how each of your five senses experiences this place.

_____

_____

_____

_____

_____

_____

_____

7 What can you do today to show appreciation to those you love? Who will you show this appreciation to?

_____

_____

_____

_____

_____

_____

_____

8 How often do you express your feelings to those you love? What can you do to show them more love?

_____

_____

_____

_____

_____

_____

_____

9 When was the last time you experienced the feeling of surprise? What about the situation made you feel that way?

_____

_____

_____

_____

_____

_____

_____

10 When was the last time someone asked you for help? Were you able to give them the help they needed? If so, how?

_____

_____

_____

_____

_____

_____

_____

11 What are your financial goals for this year? What are you doing now to reach those goals?

_____

_____

_____

_____

_____

_____

12 What are some things you have collected in your life? Do you have any current collections of specific objects?

_____

_____

_____

_____

_____

_____

13 Which people in your life generally bring you positive energy? Negative energy?

_____

_____

_____

_____

_____

_____

14 What is something good that happened to you recently that makes you realize how fortunate you are?

_____

_____

_____

_____

_____

_____

15 Describe a time when you had to choose between different paths. Do you think you made the best choice?

_____

_____

_____

_____

_____

_____

_____

16 What is your favorite day of the week? Why do you like this day? What do you do?

_____

_____

_____

_____

_____

_____

_____

17 What things do other people do that really push your buttons?

_____

_____

_____

_____

_____

_____

18 What do you think the world will look like in 100 years? Do you think it will be better or worse than it is today? Why?

_____

_____

_____

_____

_____

_____

19 Who is someone younger than you that you really admire? What are some of their best characteristics?

_____

_____

_____

_____

_____

_____

20 If you could be doing anything you want in life right now, what would you be doing?

_____

_____

_____

_____

_____

_____

_____

21 What was the worst news you ever received? How did you process that news?

_____

_____

_____

_____

_____

_____

_____

22 What are three things you can do this week to spread some happiness and positivity?

_____

_____

_____

_____

_____

_____

_____

23 Who is someone older than you that you really look up to? What are some of their best characteristics?

_____

_____

_____

_____

_____

_____

_____

24 What are some skills or knowledge you would like to learn this year? How will you acquire those skills or that knowledge?

_____

_____

_____

_____

_____

_____

_____

25 What is one of your favorite memories of being with your friends this past year?

_____

_____

_____

_____

_____

_____

26 If you were stuck on a deserted island, what one person and one object would you take with you?

_____

_____

_____

_____

_____

_____

27 Describe your day yesterday and write three good things about it.

_____

_____

_____

_____

_____

_____

_____

28 What is something you are working on now in your personal life that is helping make your life better in the future?

_____

_____

_____

_____

_____

_____

_____

29 What is a negative thought you have about yourself right now? What can you do to combat or eliminate it from your mind?

_____

_____

_____

_____

_____

_____

30 What was the last disagreement you had? How did you work through the situation?

_____

_____

_____

_____

_____

_____

31 How would you describe the past month in three words? Why did these words come to mind?

_____

_____

_____

_____

_____

_____

_____

1 How would your friends describe you? What do they love most about you?

_____

_____

_____

_____

_____

_____

2 When you are feeling sick, what or who provides comfort?

_____

_____

_____

_____

_____

_____

_____

3 Describe your current pet(s) or any pet(s) you have had in the past.

_____

_____

_____

_____

_____

_____

_____

4 What is something you would like to make more time for? What could you do this month to make that happen?

_____

_____

_____

_____

_____

_____

_____

5 Describe your first job experience. What duties did you have? Who did you work with?

_____

_____

_____

_____

_____

_____

_____

6 Do you consider yourself open-minded? What can you do to be more open-minded?

_____

_____

_____

_____

_____

_____

_____

7 Write about what is on your mind today.

_____

_____

_____

_____

_____

_____

_____

8 Do you consider yourself a risk-taker? Why or why not?

_____

_____

_____

_____

_____

_____

_____

9 What do you love most about the fall season? What are your favorite things to do?

_____

_____

_____

_____

_____

_____

_____

10 When was the last time you got out of your comfort zone? How did it make you feel?

_____

_____

_____

_____

_____

_____

_____

11 If you were given the chance to write a book about any topic or in any genre, what would you write about?

_____

_____

_____

_____

_____

_____

_____

12 Write about a time that you stood up for someone else. How did the person react to you helping them?

_____

_____

_____

_____

_____

_____

_____

13 What is one of your greatest challenges in life now? How are you handling it? Can you improve the situation by changing how you are handling it?

_____

_____

_____

_____

_____

_____

_____

14 If you could wake up and do anything you wanted tomorrow, how would you spend the day?

_____

_____

_____

_____

_____

_____

_____

15 What are three things that made you smile this week?

_____

_____

_____

_____

_____

_____

16 What was the hardest goodbye you ever had to say?

_____

_____

_____

_____

_____

_____

_____

17 Do you have any weekend rituals? Are there any rituals you would like to start?

_____

_____

_____

_____

_____

_____

18 In the past year, who have you helped through a tough situation? What did you do to help them?

_____

_____

_____

_____

_____

_____

_____

19 What does "self-care" mean to you? How do you practice self-care in your life?

_____

_____

_____

_____

_____

_____

_____

20 What is something that has been hard for you to accept in life? What do you do to be more accepting of this reality?

_____

_____

_____

_____

_____

_____

_____

21 Are you excited about this year of your life? Why or why not?

_____

_____

_____

_____

_____

_____

22 What are some of your favorite chores to do? What are some of your least favorite chores?

_____

_____

_____

_____

_____

_____

23 When was the last time you were really scared? How did you get through the situation?

_____

_____

_____

_____

_____

_____

24 What opportunity has come your way that you are grateful for?

_____

_____

_____

_____

_____

_____

_____

25 Who was your favorite teacher from school? What made them so special?

_____

_____

_____

_____

_____

_____

26 With whom do you lack self-confidence, and why do you think that is?

_____

_____

_____

_____

_____

_____

_____

27 When was the last time you felt totally at peace? Where were you and how did you feel? How could you re-create that feeling?

_____

_____

_____

_____

_____

_____

_____

28 What do you want to accomplish most in life? Are you working toward this accomplishment? Why or why not?

_____

_____

_____

_____

_____

_____

_____

29 Who is someone you wish you had a better relationship with? What could you do to improve your relationship?

_____

_____

_____

_____

_____

_____

30 What's one thing from your past that you regret? What did you learn from the experience?

_____

_____

_____

_____

_____

_____

_____

1 When was the last time you watched the sun rise or set? Describe the experience.

_____

_____

_____

_____

_____

_____

_____

2 Who have you been kind to recently? How did they feel about your kindness?

_____

_____

_____

_____

_____

_____

_____

3 What do you want your life to look like in ten years?

_____

_____

_____

_____

_____

_____

4 In what situations do you feel least confident? How do you try to improve your self-confidence in those situations?

_____

_____

_____

_____

_____

_____

_____

5 When was the last time someone extended kindness to you? How did you show your appreciation to them?

_____

_____

_____

_____

_____

_____

6 Do you find it easy to express your own feelings? Why or why not?

_____

_____

_____

_____

_____

_____

7 How do you feel about current events? What worries you? What gives you hope?

_____

_____

_____

_____

_____

_____

_____

8 What are your five best strategies for dealing with stress?

_____

_____

_____

_____

_____

_____

_____

9 Identify one area of your life you would like to improve. What are three specific actions you can take now to create change in that area?

_____

_____

_____

_____

_____

_____

_____

10 In what situations do you feel most confident? Share a specific example of when you felt confident.

_____

_____

_____

_____

_____

_____

_____

11 What's a fond memory you have from this season? What makes it special to you?

_____

_____

_____

_____

_____

_____

12 If your life was a book, how would you divide it into chapters? What would those chapters be titled?

_____

_____

_____

_____

_____

_____

_____

13 What are some things you do to procrastinate?

_____

_____

_____

_____

_____

_____

14 What is something that you tried for the first time recently? How did it go?

_____

_____

_____

_____

_____

_____

_____

15 What is one activity or habit you could remove from your daily life that would make you feel good? How can you make that change?

_____

_____

_____

_____

_____

_____

_____

16 When was the last time you asked someone for help? How did it feel to ask for help?

_____

_____

_____

_____

_____

_____

_____

17 What were your parents like when you were growing up?

_____

_____

_____

_____

_____

_____

_____

18 If you had one million dollars to give to a charity or cause of your choice, which organization would you choose? Why?

_____

_____

_____

_____

_____

_____

_____

19 What is something you want to do that you are afraid to do but would be very good for you? Why are you afraid to do it?

_____

_____

_____

_____

_____

_____

_____

20 Tell a funny story that happened to you recently.

_____

_____

_____

_____

_____

_____

_____

21 What is a skill or ability that comes easily to you? How has it helped you in life?

_____

_____

_____

_____

_____

_____

_____

22 What is something you love now that you could never have imagined liking in the past?

_____

_____

_____

_____

_____

_____

_____

23 What is something you accomplished this year that you are proud of?

_____

_____

_____

_____

_____

_____

_____

24 What is one activity or habit you could add to your daily life that would make you feel good? How can you make that happen?

_____

_____

_____

_____

_____

_____

_____

25 Write about a time when you broke someone's trust. How did you regain their trust?

_____

_____

_____

_____

_____

_____

_____

26 What TV family or family from a book is most like your own family? Why?

_____

_____

_____

_____

_____

_____

_____

27 What brings you the most worry in your life right now?

_____

_____

_____

_____

_____

_____

28 Write about one of your best friends. What makes your friendship so special, and what is it about this friend that makes them great?

_____

_____

_____

_____

_____

_____

_____

29 What do you hope future generations will learn from your generation?

_____

_____

_____

_____

_____

_____

_____

30 Has there been a time when you refused someone's help? Why was that, and do you regret it?

_____

_____

_____

_____

_____

_____

_____

31 Have you or someone close to you had a near-death experience? What was it like?

_____

_____

_____

_____

_____

_____

_____

1 What is the most exciting thing happening for you this week?

_____

_____

_____

_____

_____

_____

2 What is an area of your life that could use more organization? What could you do this month to improve the situation?

_____

_____

_____

_____

_____

_____

_____

157

3 Write about a time someone stood up for you. How did it make you feel about that person?

_____

_____

_____

_____

_____

_____

4 What have you learned about yourself this past year?

_____

_____

_____

_____

_____

_____

_____

5 Have you ever had recurring dreams? What is the common theme? If not, what sorts of things do you dream about?

_____

_____

_____

_____

_____

_____

_____

6 What is the last nice thing you bought for yourself? How did buying it make you feel?

_____

_____

_____

_____

_____

_____

_____

7 What makes you feel in control?

_____

_____

_____

_____

_____

_____

_____

8 What do you do when you do not feel in control?

_____

_____

_____

_____

_____

_____

_____

9 Share five things you love about your body.

_____

_____

_____

_____

_____

_____

_____

10 Who is someone you would like to spend more time with? How will you make time for that person this week or this month?

_____

_____

_____

_____

_____

_____

_____

11 If you could be an expert in any subject or activity, what would it be?

_____

_____

_____

_____

_____

_____

12 When was the last time you heard some happy news?

_____

_____

_____

_____

_____

_____

_____

13 How do you think other people see you when they meet you for the first time?

_____

_____

_____

_____

_____

_____

_____

14 What are the biggest hurdles you need to get over in life right now?

_____

_____

_____

_____

_____

_____

_____

15 What about the coming day are you most looking forward to?

_____

_____

_____

_____

_____

_____

16 What is the most important thing you can do today to work on this year's goals?

_____

_____

_____

_____

_____

_____

17 Do you consider yourself spontaneous? Why or why not? Where could you add more spontaneity (or more planning) in your life?

_____

_____

_____

_____

_____

_____

_____

18 What do you love about the winter months? What do you like to do during this season?

_____

_____

_____

_____

_____

_____

_____

19 What do you do to show other people your appreciation?

_____
_____
_____
_____
_____
_____
_____

20 When was the last time you had to make a tough decision? What was the outcome?

_____
_____
_____
_____
_____
_____
_____

21

What could you do this week to make someone smile?

_____

_____

_____

_____

_____

_____

22

What are five things you are grateful for today?

_____

_____

_____

_____

_____

_____

_____

NOVEMBER

23 Do you prefer to be indoors or outdoors? What do you like to do for fun in each setting?

_____

_____

_____

_____

_____

_____

24 What is one of the best things that happened in your life this year?

_____

_____

_____

_____

_____

_____

25 How do you deal with anger? How could you deal with it better?

_____

_____

_____

_____

_____

_____

26 What is the last gift you gave someone? How did they react to that gift?

_____

_____

_____

_____

_____

_____

NOVEMBER

27 Who has been there for you recently? What have they done to help you?

_____

_____

_____

_____

_____

_____

28 What are some positive strategies you use when you are feeling overwhelmed?

_____

_____

_____

_____

_____

_____

_____

29 If you did not have to work another day in your life, what would you do with your time?

_____

_____

_____

_____

_____

_____

_____

30 What is one thing you can do today to make yourself feel good? Will you do it? Why or why not?

_____

_____

_____

_____

_____

_____

_____

1 What are three long-term goals you have? What are you doing to achieve these goals?

_____

_____

_____

_____

_____

_____

2 What positive things have happened in your life this past year?

_____

_____

_____

_____

_____

_____

_____

3 List ten daily comforts that you are most grateful for.

_____

_____

_____

_____

_____

_____

4 What word or phrase would you use to summarize this past year? Why?

_____

_____

_____

_____

_____

_____

_____

5 What are three quirky things about you?

_____

_____

_____

_____

_____

_____

6 What is the most exciting thing happening this month?

_____

_____

_____

_____

_____

_____

7 Do you feel like you are aging gracefully? Why or why not?

_____

_____

_____

_____

_____

_____

8 What are some limiting beliefs you have about yourself?

_____

_____

_____

_____

_____

_____

_____

9 What do you enjoy doing when you are with friends and family?

_____

_____

_____

_____

_____

_____

_____

10 What do you spend the most money on right now?

_____

_____

_____

_____

_____

_____

_____

11 What is some feel-good news you heard recently?

_____

_____

_____

_____

_____

_____

12 How has being an introvert or an extrovert shaped your life?

_____

_____

_____

_____

_____

_____

13 Describe your favorite place in your home. What do you like about it? How does it feel to spend time in this place?

_____

_____

_____

_____

_____

_____

14 Do you have a hard time saying no? When was the last time you had to tell someone no?

_____

_____

_____

_____

_____

_____

15 What would you do in your life if you knew you could not fail?

_____

_____

_____

_____

_____

_____

16 When is the next time you get to have a day all to yourself? What will you do?

_____

_____

_____

_____

_____

_____

_____

17 What has brought a smile to your face this week?

_____

_____

_____

_____

_____

_____

_____

18 Describe a situation that you did not handle well this year. What will you do differently if you find yourself in the same situation (or a similar one)?

_____

_____

_____

_____

_____

_____

_____

19 What is something you did this past year that was rewarding? Describe how you were rewarded.

_____

_____

_____

_____

_____

_____

_____

20 Did you accomplish any of your goals in the past year? Which ones?

_____

_____

_____

_____

_____

_____

_____

_____

21
How do you celebrate the New Year, and what do you love about it?

_____

_____

_____

_____

_____

_____

22
Define what "success" means to you.

_____

_____

_____

_____

_____

_____

23
If you were told you only had one week left to live, how would you spend that time?

_____

_____

_____

_____

_____

_____

24
What is something you are looking forward to about next year?

_____

_____

_____

_____

_____

_____

25

What has been a defining moment of this past year for you? Describe it.

_____

_____

_____

_____

_____

_____

_____

26

What do you enjoy doing when you are alone?

_____

_____

_____

_____

_____

_____

_____

27 What was a life lesson you had to learn the hard way? How did it make you stronger?

_____

_____

_____

_____

_____

_____

28 What are some of your goals for the upcoming year?

_____

_____

_____

_____

_____

_____

_____

29 What is something you need to forgive yourself for? What can you do to give yourself forgiveness?

_____

_____

_____

_____

_____

_____

30 What song would describe your life right now? How does that song relate to your life?

_____

_____

_____

_____

_____

_____

31

What are ten things you are looking forward to in the future?

_____

_____

_____

_____

_____

_____

_____

Acknowledgments

I am so grateful to my husband and kids for always supporting my projects and goals. They are the best team to be on.

Thank you to my mom for being my biggest cheerleader, and to my dad, who has always encouraged me to work hard and believe in myself.

I truly have a great support system of friends and family who have encouraged me through this book journey.

About the Author

 Jaclyn Musselman is the creator of coffeepancakesanddreams.com and writes on the topics of family, motherhood, and home organization for her blog and other online parenting sites.

She is a wife and mom of one daughter and two sons, with whom she loves to create fun, lasting memories of family movie nights, Sunday pizza dinners, and a lot of road trips!

Jaclyn has a master's degree in counseling and has experience working in both school and corporate settings. As a busy mom, she knows firsthand that life can get in the way of quality self-care, so she feels it is so important to focus on gratitude and being positive every single day.

Even though she is a Midwestern girl at heart, Jaclyn dreams of living on the beach. When she is not writing or spending time with her family, she enjoys planning her next vacation, reading, and trying new recipes.

CPSIA information can be obtained
at www.ICGtesting.com
Printed in the USA
JSHW072323150223
37553JS00001B/1